Kelsey Gjesdal

A WOMAN OF EXCELLENCE

A Four-Week Study through the Book of Ruth and Proverbs 31

KELSEY GJESDAL

KELSEY LEE WRITES LLC

Introduction

The book of Ruth has been an encouragement to me for many years. If any book of the Bible could be said to be a comfort read for me, this book is it. The way Boaz and Ruth's love story unfolds always makes me smile, but there is so much more to this precious book than simply romance. It's the story of selfless love between a daughter-in-law and her mother-in-law. It's the story of a woman at her lowest, who thinks that the Almighty is against her, and she learns that God is faithful and can create beauty from ashes. And, most importantly, all Scripture is about the Word made flesh, and this story of a kinsman redeemer points to the Redeemer of our souls, Jesus Christ.

There are a few things you will need for completing this study:

- **A Bible**, preferably one you can write in. Or you can print out a copy of the book of Ruth and Proverbs 31:10-31 double-spaced, which is a great option for note taking during our study. The study guide will specifically ask you to mark the references to God in our study passages, but I encourage you to mark any other words that we focus on during our study. Marking key words with a colored pencil or a Bible highlighter will be memory aids for the future when you look back through the book of Ruth and want to quickly remember the important concepts you studied.
- **Bible highlighters or colored pencils**
- You may also want **an extra notepad or journal** for writing your prayers as we work through this study.

Let's dig into the Word together! May God's Word produce a harvest and accomplish His will in your life!

In Christ,

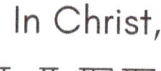

KELSEY LEE

Coffee is my go-to writing beverage!

I write Bible studies, devotionals, and teen fiction.

My favorite genre is mystery, but I also love a good fantasy or romance novel!

I love talking theology with my friends!

When I'm not working for Kelsey Lee Writes LLC, I work at a pro-life pregnancy clinic.

If I could have a backyard of just lupine, I would. I love flowers!

ABOUT THE AUTHOR

WEEK ONE:

DEVOTION

DAY 1
Ruth 1:1-7

The book of Ruth takes place during the time of the Judges. This was the period of time between when Joshua brought Israel into the Promised Land and when God began anointing kings over Israel (you can learn more about this period of time in the book of Judges). It was a time when everyone did what was right in their own eyes (Judges 21:25), which led to a lot of problems for Israel. Because of this, Israel would drift away from God, God would allow them to be invaded by enemies, they would cry out to the Lord for a deliverer, God would raise up a deliverer who would rescue Israel from their enemies and be judge over them for a time, while the judge was alive, the people would follow the Lord, and then when the judge died the people would drift away from God again. This cycle would repeat over and over until the people finally cried out to God saying they wanted a king like all the nations around them. They no longer wished for God to be their sole King.

In the middle of these cycles, we find this story about a woman named Naomi and her daughter-in-law, Ruth.

In Ruth 1:1-5, we learn that Elimelech, Naomi's husband, decided to move to Moab out of Judah because of a famine in the land. While in Moab, his two sons married Moabite women (which Israelites were not supposed to do), and all three men died. Naomi's family was gone, and all that was left were her two daughters-in-law. So, Naomi decided that she would return to the land of Judah, having heard that the Lord had provided food for His people and ended the famine (Ruth 1:6-7).

Naomi returns to the land of Judah. She is an example of repentance, of turning or returning to the ways of God.

All of us like sheep have gone astray, Each of us has turned to his own way; But the Lord has caused the iniquity of us all To fall on Him. Isaiah 53:6

All of us are like the family of Elimelech; we have all turned aside from God's ways. Everyone has tried to make their own way apart from God, and our sin has resulted in death. But thanks be to God that He has given us a way to return to Him through Jesus Christ!

The other important thing to realize is that, even when we have been saved by the blood of Christ, we still sin and need to practice repentance. Psalm 32 is a great reminder of God's love and grace toward us when we repent:

How blessed is he whose transgression is forgiven, Whose sin is covered! How blessed is the man to whom the Lord does not impute iniquity, And in whose spirit there is no deceit! When I kept silent about my sin, my body wasted away Through my groaning all day long. For day and night Your hand was heavy upon me; My vitality was drained away as with the fever heat of summer. Selah. I acknowledged my sin to You, And my iniquity I did not hide; I said, "I will confess my transgressions to the Lord"; And You forgave the guilt of my sin. Selah. Therefore, let everyone who is godly pray to You in a time when You may be found; Surely in a flood of great waters they will not reach him. You are my hiding place; You preserve me from trouble; You surround me with songs of deliverance. Selah. Psalm 32:1-7

I love how this psalm shows that God takes sin seriously, but He is also our Redeemer. In Him is forgiveness. Sometimes, as believers, we can become discouraged by the need to repent. I know for me, it is easy to start thinking, *I've been a Christian for so long, I know a lot of Scriptures, I should be better and try harder next time.* But that type of thinking forgets Psalm 32:1, "How blessed is he whose transgression is forgiven, whose sin is covered!" It's so important to remember that we will always need God's grace this side of eternity. We are saved by the blood of Christ, and through the power of the Holy Spirit (and not our own efforts) we are sanctified! Let's remember God's character and remember that He is willing to extend grace and forgiveness freely to those who repent and return to Him.

STUDY: RUTH 1:1-7

Read today's passage and mark any references to God in the passage.

Answer the following questions:

1: What brought Elimelech's family to Moab? How much time passes during these seven verses?

2: What caused Naomi to decide to return to Bethlehem?

3: Look up and record a few Scriptures that mention Bethlehem. Why is this location significant in Scripture?

4: Read Deuteronomy 7:1-6, Joshua 23:11-13, and 2 Corinthians 6:14. What commands does the Lord give to Israel and to believers in these passages? Why do you think Mahlon and Chilion married Moabite women?

5: Read Proverbs 3:5-6. In what ways have you been tempted to follow your own path instead of trusting the Lord to direct your steps?

Bonus: look up the meanings of the following names in a Bible dictionary and make note of anything interesting you learn (BlueLetterBible.org is a great place to find free Bible dictionaries!): Naomi, Elimelech, Mahlon, Chilion, Orpah, Ruth, Moab, and Bethlehem.

DAY 2
Ruth 1:8-13

Scripture zooms in on Naomi in today's passage, revealing the brokenness of a woman who has been through tremendous loss and pain. It is easy to look at Naomi and judge her for the bitterness dripping from her words and actions. But Naomi is displaying a very real and raw response to grief. She is weeping, and she wrestles with feeling that the Lord's hand is against her. No doubt, she probably feels this way because she knows that she and her husband should not have left the Promised Land during the famine.

She begins by urging her daughters-in-law to return to the homes of their mothers. This shows Naomi's concern for the well-being of her daughters-in-law; she knew they ought to remarry and have a future in life that she could not provide for them. But we see here that Ruth and Orpah desire to return to Bethlehem with Naomi. Something in Naomi and her family had impressed these two young women enough that they desired to go with this woman, even in her sorrow and depression. We catch a glimpse at the relationship Naomi must have had with these women, one that placed in them a desire to be with Naomi's people.

But Naomi insists that there is no hope for them if they stay with her. She cannot provide them with husbands, with a future. She wants them to have a future, and she believes, in her grief, that they will have no future if they go with her because "the hand of the Lord has gone forth against me" (Ruth 1:13). Naomi has recognized that she and her household had sinned against the Lord by not trusting Him to provide for them during a famine, but even though she is now returning to the Promised Land, Naomi is convinced that the Lord is still against her.

8.

During times of sorrow, we often cry out as the psalmist, "my God, my God, why have you forsaken me?" (Ps. 22:1). We question God's goodness and His sovereignty, wondering why He allows bad things to happen when it seems like we have done nothing to deserve the trials we face. Or, like Naomi, we can see how our disobedience to God has led to a time of sorrow, and we are tempted to believe that the Lord's hand will forever be against us because of our sin. But, in her grief, Naomi was forgetting the important truth that there is forgiveness with the Lord (Ps. 130:4), and that godly sorrow is meant to lead us to the repentance that leads to life (2 Cor. 7:10).

Another note to make about this passage is that when Naomi says, "it is harder for me than for you," the Hebrew word she uses here that is translated "harder" is mārar, or "to make bitter."[1] (We will see this come back up again later in the chapter when Naomi tells the women of Judah to call her Mara, or bitter.) This bitterness that Naomi is experiencing is not only that her husband and sons have died, but that the sins of herself and her family have affected not only her but also her daughters-in-law. Certainly, Ruth and Orpah were experiencing deep grief over the loss of their husbands. I'm sure they were questioning God's hand in their lives, too. But Naomi was dealing with the consequences of her own actions on her life and the lives of those around her. Orpah and Ruth were experiencing the consequences of other people's sin on their lives. As we go through life, we will find ourselves in Naomi's shoes, finding the consequences of our sin impacting our lives and the lives of those around us. And we will find ourselves in Ruth and Orpah's shoes, experiencing the pain that comes from living in a sin-cursed world. Regardless of what we are experiencing, what we can fall on in these difficult circumstances is the love and sovereignty of God. We can trust that He loves His children and can work what was meant for evil for good (Gen. 50:20), and we can trust that one day all wrongs will be made right at Christ's second coming (Rev. 21).

As we continue our study, we will watch Naomi find healing from her grief with time. We will see how, accompanied by a daughter-in-law who loves her selflessly, Naomi's faith returns and is strengthened as God miraculously provides for these two women. Naomi will see that the hand of the Lord is not against her forever.

My son, do not reject the discipline of the Lord Or loathe His reproof, For whom the Lord loves He reproves, Even as a father corrects the son in whom he delights. Proverbs 3:11-12

The hand of the Lord was not against Naomi as one would come against an enemy. The Lord, as a good Father, disciplines His children in order to help them mature. It is the love of God that motivates His discipline in response to our sin.

1: "H4843 - mārar - Strong's Hebrew Lexicon (kjv)." Blue Letter Bible. Accessed 10 Feb, 2025. https://www.blueletterbible.org/lexicon/h4843/kjv/wlc/0-1/

STUDY: RUTH 1:8-13

Read today's passage and mark any references to God in the passage.

Answer the following questions:

1: What instructions does Naomi giver her daughters-in-law, and what reasons does she give for insisting they return to their fathers' houses?

2: Read Psalm 130. What does this psalm teach about God's response to our sin? How does this connect to Naomi's story?

3: What two blessings does Naomi pray for her daughters-in-law?

4: Read the following passages and note what they teach about God's kindness and about rest: Psalm 23:2; Psalm 57:10; Psalm 69:16; Psalm 98:3; Psalm 107:15; Psalm 116:7; Isaiah 54:10; Jeremiah 31:3; Matthew 11:28-29.

5: Read Revelation 21. What hope does this passage give for difficult times?

DAY 3
Ruth 1:14-18

After Naomi decided to return to Bethlehem, she tells her daughters-in-law to return to their families instead of going with her (see Ruth 1:6-13). Orpah listens to her mother-in-law and goes back to her family, but Ruth had a different response.

And they lifted up their voices and wept again; and Orpah kissed her mother-in-law, but Ruth clung to her. Then she said, "Behold, your sister-in-law has gone back to her people and her gods; return after your sister-in-law." But Ruth said, "Do not urge me to leave you or turn back from following you; for where you go, I will go, and where you lodge, I will lodge. Your people shall be my people, and your God, my God. Where you die, I will die, and there I will be buried. Thus may the Lord do to me, and worse, if anything but death parts you and me." When she saw that she was determined to go with her, she said no more to her. Ruth 1:14-18

Ruth made a covenant with Naomi to stay with her.

What is a covenant? The Hebrew word for covenant is bᵉrîyth, which means a compact or alliance in the form of a cutting, signified by a sign or pledge.[1] This is displayed well in Genesis 15 when the Lord makes a covenant with Abram, promising to make him the father of a great nation. God gave a sign of His promise to Abram by having Abram cut in half several animals for an offering, and then the Lord walked between these offerings as a burning torch to signify His pledge. This symbolized that, should He break His Word, Abram could do to Him what had been done to the animals. What makes this account with Abram so significant is that God passed through the offering twice, once for Himself and once for Abram. Abram couldn't keep

1: "H1285 - bᵉrîṭ - Strong's Hebrew Lexicon (nasb95)." Blue Letter Bible. Accessed 30 Jan, 2025. https://www.blueletterbible.org/lexicon/h1285/nasb95/wlc/0-1/

his end of the covenant, to be blameless before the Lord all his days, and God knew that. God knew we couldn't do that, either. So, the Lord took upon Himself the weight of Abram's side of the bargain--if Abram couldn't keep the covenant, the Lord would be cut in two on his behalf. And that is exactly what happened when the Lord Jesus Christ died on the cross in our place. He fulfilled the Abrahamic Covenant when Abraham, and the whole world, could not.

Covenants are powerful promises with serious consequences. When Ruth tells Naomi, "thus may the Lord do to me and worse if anything but death parts you and me," she was signifying the solemn oath of her covenant. She pledged to be faithful to Naomi and her God, and, as we will see through the rest of this study, Ruth keeps her covenant to Naomi.

Ruth was a woman of excellence (see Ruth 3:11), and a huge part of that was her devotion to her family. She was trustworthy and did her mother-in-law good by going with her and caring for her.

As Christian women, we must ask ourselves what are we devoted to? Are we devoted first to the Lord? Are we devoted to our families? To our husbands (Proverbs 31:12 says, "she does him good and not evil all the days of her life," so that means even when we're single, we can be trustworthy toward our husband, even when we don't know who he is)?

Ruth was devoted to her mother-in-law, and when she declared her covenant with Naomi, she also declared her choice to be devoted to, or in covenant with, the Lord.

A woman of excellence makes a covenant with God, to be His daughter and to follow wherever He leads. And she makes a covenant with her family, to be trustworthy and do good for them all her days. A covenant is serious; it's meant to be an unbreakable promise, something not taken lightly. What kind of covenants have you or will you choose to make?

I hope the example of Ruth is encouraging to you. May we pursue being women of excellence and women in covenant with God through God's strength!

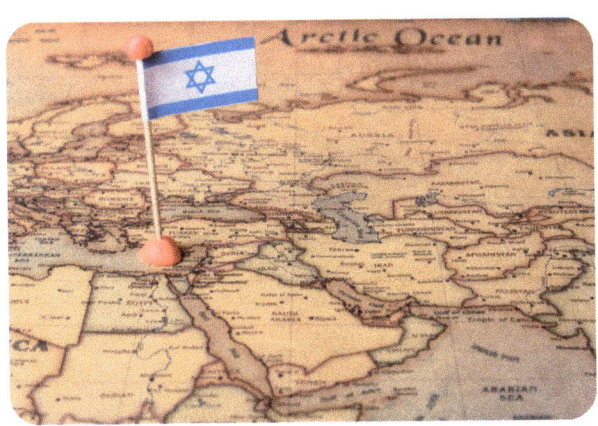

STUDY: RUTH 1:14-18

Read today's passage and mark any references to God in the passage.

Answer the following questions:

1: List the promises Ruth made to Naomi in today's passage. How does understanding biblical covenants change your perception of Ruth's words to Naomi?

2: Read Genesis 9:11-17. What do you learn about God and covenants from this passage?

3: Read Numbers 30:1-2, Ecclesiastes 5:4, and Matthew 5:37. What does the Bible teach regarding keeping our word? How does this apply to Ruth and the covenant she made with Naomi?

4: As Christians, we have entered into covenant with God by placing our faith in the Lord Jesus. the signs of our covenant are the Lord's Supper and baptism. Take some time to reflect on what you have learned about covenants today and how that impacts your life as a follower of Christ.

5: Read Proverbs 31:10-12. How does Ruth display these qualities of an excellent woman?

Bonus: Look up the following covenants God made with His people - the Noahic Covenant, the Abrahamic Covenant, the Mosaic Covenant, and the Davidic Covenant. What signs did God give to seal these covenants? How do they point to Jesus?

DAY 4
Ruth 1:19-22

Ruth and Naomi make their way to Bethlehem, which means the House of Bread.[1] In verse 21, Naomi says, "I went out full, but the Lord has brought me back empty." What an interesting lament. She left from the House of Bread full. She returns to the House of Bread empty, needing to be filled. How tempting it is for us to seek fulfillment and satisfaction in whatever shiny promise the world allures us with. But the allurements of the world will never satisfy us. Only in Christ will we find the Bread of Life to satisfy us for all eternity.

Let's also note that when Naomi went out from Bethlehem, it was because of a famine. The House of Bread, ironically, wasn't living up to it's name. Remember, the book of Ruth takes place during the times of the Judges when everyone did what was right in his own eyes (Judges 21:25). Over and over again, Israel would stray from the Lord and bring upon themselves the judgment that the Lord had promised they would face if they were not faithful to their covenant (Joshua 24:14-28). Then, the Lord would have mercy on them and raise up a deliverer who would judge Israel, and for a time they would return to the Lord, then, after the judge died, the cycle would repeat. Likely, the famine in Bethlehem was during a rebellious point in these cycles. So, not only did Naomi's family get lured away from God's ways, so did Israel.

We see again here the heart of Naomi broken over the loss she has experienced. She tells the women of Israel to no longer call her Naomi, a name meaning pleasant.[2] She requests to be called Mara, which, as we learned before, means bitter. Naomi is processing her grief and bitterness, feeling that the Almighty has dealt her a bitter hand. While her previous words to

14.

1: "H1035 - bêṯ leḥem - Strong's Hebrew Lexicon (nasb95)." Blue Letter Bible. Accessed 11 Feb, 2025. https://www.blueletterbible.org/lexicon/h1035/nasb95/wlc/0-1/
2: "H5281 - nāʿŏmî - Strong's Hebrew Lexicon (nasb95)." Blue Letter Bible. Accessed 12 Feb, 2025. https://www.blueletterbible.org/lexicon/h5281/nasb95/wlc/0-1/

Ruth acknowledged that she was experiencing the consequences of her own choices, at this point she is now expressing bitterness toward God and blaming Him for her pain. This is a normal part of the grieving process. Anger and depression are common responses to loss, and wondering why the Almighty God, who is sovereign over all, allows heart-wrenching pain is a question everyone grapples with at some point in life.

Job wrestled with these questions after losing everything he had, his health, and all his children. He begged for an audience with God so that he could make his case and receive an answer from the Almighty (Job 31:35). We know from the opening chapter of Job that he was a righteous man before God and that Satan had challenged God, saying that Job would deny Him if God allowed hardship into his life. God allows Satan to touch Job's life, and Satan is proved wrong as Job remains faithful to the Lord. But Job didn't know about what had happened in heaven, and even though he remained faithful to God, he still wrestled with questions of God's justice and goodness in his present situation. In Job 38, God finally answers Job, but not in the way we would expect. God doesn't give Job a play-by-play of what went down in heaven. Instead, He tells Job of His power over creation. He asks Job to explain to Him the mysteries of the universe, which Job cannot. And Job leaves this discussion humbled before the Lord, for now he has truly understood the magnitude of the Almighty God (Job 42:1-6).

We may not always know or see why God allows different hardships into our lives. Sometimes, like Joseph in Genesis 50, we can look back on difficult times and see that God used them to bring about good. Other times, like Job, we may never know the reason behind God allowing hardships in our lives. But we can trust that He is good and just, no matter what. God does not cause the evil that happens in our lives, but in His wisdom He allows it, whether it be the consequences of our (or others') sin or the result of spiritual warfare, in order to grow us in Christ-likeness and to bring glory to His name. Whether we know the reason behind our suffering or we never understand, God is forever worthy of our praise.

At this point, Naomi is at her lowest. She is depressed and angry. But her story does not end here. Over the next few chapters we will see that Naomi not only finds healing, but through her testimony the Lord is given praise. God will create beauty from the ashes in her life. But right now, in chapter one, she is grieving and in pain. And the Lord is walking with her through the midst of her suffering. He is near to her broken heart.

The Lord is near to the brokenhearted And saves those who are crushed in spirit. Psalm 34:18

STUDY: RUTH 1:19-22

Read today's passage and mark any references to God in the passage.

Answer the following questions:

1: What observations do you make in this passage? People, places, times?

2: Naomi expresses her grief in bitterness toward God. Have you ever experienced similar feelings? Read the following Scriptures: Psalm 34:18; Psalm 51:17; Psalm 147:3; Matthew 26:37-42; 2 Corinthians 1:3-7; 1 Thessalonians 4:13-14. What do these passages teach us about grief?

3: Read Job 1:20-22, Job 19:25, and Job 42:1-6. How does Job respond to his trials and to the Lord in these passages? What can we learn about grieving from Job?

4: Write out a prayer to the Lord reflecting on whatever today's study has brought to mind for you. Remember, when we draw near to God, He draws near to us (James 4:8).

Bonus: Read the whole book of Ruth, watching Naomi's progression of healing from grief. What do you learn about healing from grief through this book?

DAY 5

Review Ruth 1:1-22

Read Ruth 1:1-22 and Proverbs 31:10-31 and spend some time meditating on the following questions:

1: What have I learned about God this week?

2: How does this chapter point to the gospel?

3: What have I learned about godly womanhood this week?

4: What has the Lord revealed to me through this chapter about how I ought to live?

5: How can I apply what I have learned from this chapter in this next week?

6: Journal a prayer to the Lord.

But Ruth said, "Do not urge me to leave you or turn back from following you; for where you go, I will go, and where you lodge, I will lodge. Your people shall be my people, and your God, my God.

Ruth 1:16

DEVOTION

WEEK TWO: DILIGENCE

DAY 1
Ruth 2:1-7

Our study now comes to the second chapter of Ruth, and through this chapter we will see an example of a woman of diligence.

In Ruth 2, Ruth decided to go out and glean in the fields in order to take care of herself and Naomi (Ruth 2:1-3). One of God's laws for the Israelites was to leave the corners of their fields for the needy to glean from (Lev. 19:9-10). So, in accordance with the provision God had for them, Ruth went out and gleaned barley among the fields and happened to come into Boaz's field (Ruth 2:3).

I love how the Bible says she "happened" to come to Boaz's field. The story of Ruth really shows how even in what seems like a coincidence, God is at work! This concept of God's hand orchestrating the events of our lives is termed by theologians as God's providence. Ruth doesn't know the future; she is simply being obedient to what the Lord has called her to for the present. And God is divinely orchestrating her movements to bring her into contact with Boaz.

We learn from Ruth 2 that Boaz is a godly man. He wishes the Lord's blessing on the reapers, and they in turn wish God's blessing upon him (verse 4). There appears to be great respect between Boaz and his workers. We also see that Boaz is a man of wealth, as he has a profitable farming business going. Later in the book of Ruth, we will learn that Boaz sat among the elders at the gate and that he is a relative of Naomi.

To be known in the gate was an important position for Boaz. Esteemed and honored men sat at the gate, and the gate functioned as the courtroom, a place to conduct business, and a public meeting place.[1] Boaz is an esteemed man of Bethlehem, and it is to this man's field that the Lord has directed Ruth.

Boaz notices Ruth right away and asks who she is. He learns that this is Ruth, the Moabite who returned with Naomi. She requested permission to glean in Boaz's fields and had been working since morning (Ruth 2:6-7). Here we witness Ruth's example of diligence. We will find later that Ruth gleans in the field until evening (Ruth 2:17). She put in a full day's work to provide for herself and her mother-in-law.

It can be tempting to view work as a bad thing or a necessary evil of life. After all, God did curse the ground and say that work would be hard as a consequence of man's sin (see Genesis 3:17). However, work was instituted *before* the Fall. God had commanded Adam and Eve to cultivate and keep the garden while they were still living in perfection (Genesis 2:15). As image bearers of God, work is one of the ways that we reflect His image in the world. God worked six days and rested on the seventh (Genesis 2:2). In the same way, the Lord calls us to rhythms of rest and work. Work is meant to be a blessing from God, and while work has been affected by the consequences of our sin, it is still a good gift from God that should be stewarded well. And Ruth stewarded her work well. So well, in fact, that Boaz takes note.

When you are working, whether it be at school, your job, or home responsibilities, how are you stewarding your work? Are you working with diligence? Does your diligence flow from a heart desiring to glorify God in all you do?

Whatever you do, do your work heartily, as for the Lord rather than for men, Colossians 3:23

Whether, then, you eat or drink or whatever you do, do all to the glory of God. 1 Corinthians 10:31

May our work always be done with diligence to the praise of God's glory!

> **Diligence:**
> "steady, earnest, and energetic effort : devoted and painstaking work and application to accomplish an undertaking."[2]

1: Guzik, D. "Study Guide for Ruth 4 by David Guzik." Blue Letter Bible. Last Modified 6/2022. https://www.blueletterbible.org/comm/guzik_david/study-guide/ruth/ruth-4.cfm

2: "Definition of DILIGENCE." n.d. Www.merriam-Webster.com. https://www.merriam-webster.com/dictionary/diligence.

STUDY: RUTH 2:1-7

Read today's passage and mark any references to God in the passage.

Answer the following questions:

1: What do you learn about the character of Boaz and Ruth in these verses?

2: Read Proverbs 6:6-11, Proverbs 10:4, and Proverbs 21:5. What do these passages teach about diligence?

3: Read Leviticus 19:9-10. What do you learn about God's character from this passage? In Acts 6, we learn that the early church took care of their widows by providing them with food. How might our churches today practically take care of those in need?

4: Read Psalm 90:17, Ephesians 4:28, Colossians 3:22-24, and 2 Thessalonians 3:10. How can we display the gospel in our work?

Bonus: Boaz and his servants greet one another with a benediction, or a phrase of blessing. Look up other benedictions in Scripture (some examples include Numbers 6:24-26; Romans 15:13; Ephesians 3:17-19). What do you learn about blessing one another through studying these benedictions?

DAY 2
Ruth 2:8-16

We left off with Boaz inquiring about the young woman gleaning in his field. He is impressed by Ruth's diligence, and he goes to speak to her. He tells Ruth to stay in his fields to reap where she will be safe and provided for. In fact, Boaz goes out of his way to tell the reapers to leave extra grain for Ruth to gather. Throughout the book of Ruth, we see Boaz, who is Ruth's kinsman redeemer, display character traits that point to our ultimate Redeemer, Jesus. Here, we see Boaz displaying protection and provision for Ruth. Christ also gives protection and provision to His church:

And my God will supply all your needs according to His riches in glory in Christ Jesus. Philippians 4:19

But the Lord is faithful, and He will strengthen and protect you from the evil one. 2 Thessalonians 3:3

Ruth asks Boaz why he's showing her kindness. After all, she is a foreigner in the land, from an enemy country of Israel no less. As we learned before, the Lord had commanded his people not to intermarry with foreign women because they might draw them away from faith in God. It's possible that Ruth was not looked on favorably by most Israelites, as she was not only from an enemy country but her deceased husband had broken the commandment of God when he married her.

But Boaz tells Ruth that he has heard about her kindness to her mother-in-law and how she came with Naomi from her homeland to a country that was foreign to her. He knew she had chosen to serve the Lord. Boaz prays a blessing for her, that God would provide for her as she has come to seek refuge from Him.

Ruth's reputation and care for Naomi has preceded her, and that reputation will be proven true as she continues to glean in Boaz's field until evening, beat out her grain, and return to Naomi with an ephah of barley (Ruth 2:17). An ephah of barley weighed about forty pounds—that's a lot of hard work![1] Ruth, once again, proves herself to be a woman of diligence.

It's also interesting to note that Boaz's father was Salmon (Ruth 4:20). Salmon was the husband of Rahab, the harlot who saved the spies who were sent to scope out Jericho in Joshua 2. She, like Ruth, was a foreign woman who came to fear the Lord. She married an Israelite, and she, like Ruth, was in the lineage of Christ! Through the stories of these women, we see that the Lord did not command Israel not to marry foreigners because Israel was somehow a superior people group. The command to not marry foreign women was because God knew that when a believer marries an unbeliever, it creates an unequally yoked marriage, and often the believing spouse will be pulled into sin by the unbelieving spouse. In the New Testament, this concept is reiterated in the context of the church; believers are free to marry whomever they choose so long as they are marrying another believer (see 1 Corinthians 7:39 and 2 Corinthians 6:14).

Two more character qualities Ruth demonstrates in this passage are humility and respect. She treats Boaz with honor as the owner of the field in which she is working and humbly receives his kind words with gratitude. When we feign humility and don't receive someone's kind words with gratitude, we do them a disservice. It is not humble to respond to someone's kindness with self-deprecating statements. Ruth demonstrates a godly response to praise by acknowledging Boaz for his kind words that have comforted her while acknowledging her station in life.

We live in a culture that doesn't practice respect. We don't listen to one another and show deference to one another as we ought. But Ruth showed respect in how she spoke to Boaz; she used a title of respect for him, and she honored him for his position. When we treat others with respect, we are demonstrating that we understand that people are made in the image of God and as such deserve to be treated with dignity. When we treat others with respect, we are in turn showing respect to the Creator.

1: National Bible Bee. Redeemed: Primary answer anchor. 2022. Retrieved from cdn.biblebee.org/wp-content/uploads/2022/05/23182115/DJ22_Primary_Teacher.pdf p. 34

STUDY: RUTH 2:8-16

Read today's passage and mark any references to God in the passage.

Answer the following questions:

1: How does Boaz demonstrate care for Ruth? How does this point to Jesus, our ultimate Kinsman Redeemer?

2: How does Ruth respond to the kindness of Boaz? What can we learn from her example?

3: Read Psalm 46 and Psalm 62. What do these passages teach about God as our refuge?

4: Read Leviticus 19:15, Leviticus 19:32, Romans 12:10, Romans 13:7, and 1 Peter 2:17. What do these passages teach about respect for others?

Bonus: Read Joshua 2, Joshua 6:22-25, Matthew 1:5, and Hebrews 11:31. What do you learn about God from Rahab's story? How might Rahab's story have affected Boaz?

DAY 3
Ruth 2:17-23

Ruth finishes up her full day of gleaning and returns to her mother-in-law with an ephah of barley. Remember, that was about forty pounds of barley, so it's understandable that Naomi would ask Ruth where she had worked and would bless whoever had taken notice of her. The Lord had provided for them and satisfied them, just as He did for Abraham when God provided the ram in the thicket (Genesis 22), and just as God provides for us and satisfies our soul hunger in Christ our Savior.

Ruth tells Naomi that the man who took notice of her was Boaz, and Naomi gets excited. Boaz is a relative, and a close relative at that. Naomi knew that the Lord had commanded relatives to take care of their family, and God had providentially guided Ruth to the field of a family member who would care for them. In chapter two, we see Naomi beginning to feel hope once again. The God of Heaven has not utterly forsaken her; He is providing for her above and beyond what she expected through the hand of Boaz.

Naomi gives Ruth practical advice for staying in Boaz's fields as he is an upright man and will offer her protection. She might not experience that same kind of protection if she were to glean in other fields. This is a good reminder to be prudent and wise with where we are and who we are with.

So, Ruth stays in Boaz's field through the barley and the wheat harvest, "and she lived with her mother-in-law" (Ruth 2:23). She stuck by her covenant to Naomi. She promised to lodge where Naomi lodged. Ruth demonstrates selfless love to this older woman. Surely, she could've been out seeking a husband (which Boaz takes note of in the next chapter!), but she chose to stay with Naomi, to provide for her, and to dwell with her. She put the needs of another above her own.

We see this same kind of selfless love demonstrated at the cross. The Lord made a covenant with His people, that He would provide for us a Redeemer to crush the head of the serpent (Gen. 3:15). Two-thousand years ago God fulfilled His covenant by sending His only begotten Son, Jesus Christ, into the world. As Jonathan Edwards once said, "You contribute nothing to your salvation except the sin that made it necessary."[1] We do not deserve God's grace and love. We do not deserve Christ's sacrificial death on the cross to pay the penalty for our sin. Yet Christ, out of love for the Heavenly Father and love for His bride (the church), chose to go to the cross. He died in our place and rose from the grave three days later, gaining the victory over sin and death for all those who call on His name. This is the most selfless act of love in human history. And this selfless love is what we are called to imitate as Christians.

Have this attitude in yourselves which was also in Christ Jesus, who, although He existed in the form of God, did not regard equality with God a thing to be grasped, but emptied Himself, taking the form of a bond-servant, and being made in the likeness of men. Being found in appearance as a man, He humbled Himself by becoming obedient to the point of death, even death on a cross. Philippians 2:5-8

Selfless love requires humility and regarding others as more important than ourselves (Philippians 2:3). Ruth demonstrated this in her care for Naomi, and we are called to show selfless love to those in our lives as well. May we be women who walk in the love and humility of Christ.

1: Curt Blattman, "Jonathan Edwards – Quotes to Ponder – Bible Apologetics – a DAILY DEVOTIONAL," Bible Apologetics – A DAILY DEVOTIONAL, July 10, 2023, https://bibleapologetics.org/jonathan-edwards-quotes-to-ponder/.

Kelsey Gjesdal

STUDY: RUTH 2:17-23

Read today's passage and mark any references to God in the passage.

Answer the following questions:

1: What do you learn about Ruth, Naomi, and Boaz from this passage?

2: Ruth is continuing to keep the covenant she made to Naomi. What stands out to you about her commitment to this promise?

3: Read Philippians 2:1-11. What does this passage teach you about Christ? What does this passage teach you about love?

4: Read Genesis 22. How does God show Himself to be a provider for Abraham in this passage? How does He show Himself to be a provider for Ruth and Naomi?

Bonus: Do a word study on The Lord Will Provide (Gen. 22:14). What is the Hebrew name for God our Provider? (You can look this up using BlueLetterBible.org.) Where else in Scripture is God called our provider? How does understanding God as Provider impact your understanding of God's providence in Ruth and Naomi's lives?

DAY 4
Proverbs 31:13-22

We've been looking this week at the diligence of Ruth. In Proverbs 31, a mother is telling her son what kind of woman he ought to marry, and one primary characteristic of a godly woman is a woman of diligence.

The Proverbs 31 woman is hard working and takes good care of her household, just like Ruth did for Naomi (Prov. 31:13-15, 18-19). She is wise with her money (Prov. 31:16). She is diligent to take care of her body (Prov. 31:17). She takes care of the poor and needy, exemplifying selfless love as Ruth did (Prov. 31:20). Because she is wise with her money and works hard to take care of herself and her family, she does not fear the changing seasons (Prov. 31:21-22).

One description of the Proverbs 31 woman that I love is that she "works with her hands in delight" (Prov. 31:13). She works diligently, not because she has to, but with delight. Ruth was this kind of woman. She provided for herself and Naomi, she was wise, and she took care of Naomi. She did this with love in her heart for her mother-in-law.

As daughters of God, we have the opportunity to work with our hands in delight, to be diligent in whatever we do. This doesn't mean that we will love every single job or responsibility we have, but when we fix our eyes on the Lord and do our work as unto Christ, we can work with delight at any job before us, whether that be working a dream job, changing diapers and folding laundry, or working a job that we don't love. We work diligently to bring glory to God, because we delight in serving the Lord. Diligence in our work, but also the attitude we have while working, matters to God.

As we take a look at Proverbs 31 today, I want you to keep in mind the context of this chapter. This chapter has often been used as a legalistic checklist for what a godly woman is supposed to look like. (For example, if you're not sewing your own clothes, you're not a real Proverbs 31 woman.) However, this chapter is written from a mother to her son. Verses 1-9 are instructions for what kind of king this mother wants her son to be, and verses 10-31 are instructions on what type of woman she wants him to marry. She implores him to marry an excellent wife. But what is an excellent wife? This chapter was not a step-by-step checklist for being an excellent wife, but rather principles of the godly character a king should seek in a future wife. And ultimately, the excellent wife is a woman who fears the Lord.

Of course, this chapter can, and should be, applied to us as women. We should study it and look for the principles of godly character outlined in this beautiful chapter. But it's important to keep the context in mind and to remember that ultimately what we should desire to be are women who fear God. Our godly character will flow from that foundation.

Again, this chapter is not a checklist for how to be a godly woman. It's an example of a woman with godly character traits. These traits are:
·Trustworthy (11-12)
·Good work ethic (13-14, 18-19)
·Caring of her family (15, 21, 27)
·Wise with her money (16, 24)
·Takes care of her body (17)
·Generous (20)
·Doesn't worry about the future (21, 25)
·Dignified (25)
·Speaks with wisdom and kindness (26)
·Fears the Lord (30)

There are many women in the Bible who exemplify this type of character, including Ruth. But the main trait from which all the other traits flow is the fear of the Lord. May we, like Ruth, be women who fear the Lord and live out of our reverence for and devotion to Him.

STUDY: PROVERBS 31:13-22

Read Proverbs 31:13-22, 30 and mark any references to God in the passage.

Answer the following questions:

1: What are the character qualities of the Proverbs 31 woman? Which characteristics do you see in Ruth?

2: Read the following verses: Proverbs 1:7, Proverbs 9:10, Proverbs 14:27, Proverbs 15:33, Proverbs 19:23, and Proverbs 23:17. What insight do these passages give you about a godly woman?

3: What do you learn about work ethic from Proverbs 31? How might it look to work with your hands in delight in your own daily responsibilities?

4: Who in your life exemplifies the Proverbs 31 woman? (Remember, it doesn't mean someone who lives by the Proverbs 31 checklist but rather lives out the godly character traits of the Proverbs 31 woman in today's context.)

DAY 5

Review Ruth 2:1-23

Read Ruth 2:1-23 and Proverbs 31:10-31 and spend some time meditating on the following questions:

1: What have I learned about God this week?

2: How does this chapter point to the gospel?

3: What have I learned about godly womanhood this week?

4: What has the Lord revealed to me through this chapter about how I ought to live?

5: How can I apply what I have learned from this chapter in this next week?

6: Journal a prayer to the Lord.

> Boaz replied to her, "All that you have done for your mother-in-law after the death of your husband has been fully reported to me, and how you left your father and your mother and the land of your birth, and came to a people that you did not previously know. May the Lord reward your work, and your wages be full from the Lord, the God of Israel, under whose wings you have come to seek refuge." Ruth 2:11-12

DILIGENCE

WEEK THREE: REPUTATION

DAY 1
Ruth 3:1-5

Ruth 3 begins with Naomi hatching a plan. Naomi really wants Ruth to find a husband, but not just any husband--they need a redeemer (more on that next week!). And Boaz seems to be the perfect candidate. Ruth has been working in his fields for the barley and wheat harvests, which means she's had some time to get to know his character.

Naomi tells Ruth to wash and dress up, go to the threshing floor, and lie down at Boaz's feet when he goes to sleep; then Boaz would tell her what to do (Ruth 3:3-4). Some people take this passage to mean that Naomi was instructing Ruth to be inappropriate in her behavior toward Boaz, but that is not the case. David Guzik explains the cultural significance in his commentary:

> "At the appropriate time, Naomi instructs Ruth to **go in, uncover his feet, and lie down.** Some might think this was a provocative gesture, as if Ruth was told to provocatively offer herself sexually to Boaz. This was not how this gesture was understood in that day. In the culture of that day, this was understood as an act of total submission. In that day, this was understood to be the role of a servant — to lay at their master's feet and be ready for any command of the master. So, when Naomi told Ruth to **lie down** at Boaz's feet, she told her to come to him in a totally humble, submissive way. Don't lose sight of the larger picture: Ruth came to claim a right. Boaz was her *goel*, her kinsman-redeemer, and she had the right to expect him to marry her and raise up a family to perpetuate the name of Elimelech. But Naomi wisely counseled Ruth to not come as a victim demanding her rights, but as a humble servant, trusting in the goodness of her kinsman-redeemer. She said to Boaz, 'I respect you, I trust you, and I put my fate in your hands.' **He will tell you what you should do:** Of course, this was a situation that had

the potential for disaster if Boaz should mistreat Ruth in some way. But Naomi and Ruth had the chance to get to know Boaz, and they knew what kind of man he was — a good man, a godly man, one to whom Ruth could confidently submit."[1]

Ruth responds to Naomi's plan with submission; she follows Naomi's instructions to a T. Ruth trusts Naomi and listens to her counsel. Ruth was willing to take a risk.

Something to note about Ruth throughout her life is her willingness to take risks. She took a risk when she left Moab and went to Bethlehem with Naomi. She was willing to go out and glean in the fields even though there were potential dangers. And she took a risk to follow Naomi's instructions and ask Boaz to be her kinsman redeemer. But with every risk she took, Ruth was following the Lord. She chose the God of Israel as her God when she went to Bethlehem. She chose to trust God's law that the corners of the fields were for her and her mother-in-law to glean and be provided for. And she trusted God's laws when she went to ask Boaz to be her kinsman redeemer. The hand of God had provided for her needs so far; now she was trusting God to provide her a redeemer.

A woman of excellence is willing to take risks when the Lord calls her to. Note the "when God calls her to" part. You should never take risks that don't glorify God. God may call us to do things that seem scary. He may call us to give up things that are hard to give up. We may have no clue how our surrender to the Lord will turn out. But we do know that we can trust the Lord because He is good. He is faithful. He is our provider. Whatever He calls us to, He will provide us with what we need to accomplish His will. And that includes the confidence we need to step out in faith, not because we have all the answers but because we trust His character.

In the fear of the Lord there is strong confidence, And his children will have refuge. Proverbs 14:26

Reputation:
"1: overall quality or character as seen or judged by people in general; recognition by other people of some characteristic or ability; 2: a place in public esteem or regard."[2]

1: Guzik, D. "Study Guide for Ruth 3 by David Guzik." ©1996-present The Enduring Word Bible Commentary by David Guzik – enduringword.com. Used with permission.
2: "Definition of REPUTATION." n.d. Www.merriam-Webster.com. https://www.merriam-webster.com/dictionary/reputation.

STUDY: RUTH 3:1-5

Read today's passage and mark any references to God in the passage.

Answer the following questions:

1: What instructions did Naomi give to Ruth? Why do you think she desires security for Ruth?

2: What character traits has Boaz demonstrated so far in the book of Ruth? How might his character have given Ruth confidence in obeying Naomi's instructions?

3: Read the following verses: Psalm 71:5, Acts 4:13, and Hebrews 13:6. What do these verses teach about confidence?

4: Ruth took risks in order to follow the Lord. Who else in Scripture can you think of who took risks in order to follow the Lord? List three examples and what you learn about following the Lord from their lives.

Bonus: Research what the process of winnowing barley would have been like in Boaz's day. What insight does this process give you to the story and why Boaz is sleeping at the threshing floor?

DAY 2
Ruth 3:6–13

Naomi tells Ruth to go to Boaz and ask him to be their kinsman redeemer. Ruth listens to her mother-in-law and takes a risk, and Boaz responds. In the middle of the night, Boaz wakes up and realizes that Ruth is lying at his feet, and she asks him to be a protector for herself since he is a close relative (Ruth 3:9). Take a look at Boaz's response:

Then he said, "May you be blessed of the Lord, my daughter. You have shown your last kindness to be better than the first by not going after young men, whether poor or rich. Now, my daughter, do not fear. I will do for you whatever you ask, for all my people in the city know that you are a woman of excellence. Ruth 3:10–11

God is again extending his hand of mercy through Boaz. But notice Boaz's commendation of Ruth's character. He says that everyone in the city knows she is a woman of excellence. Her reputation has preceded her, and it's a very good reputation. We're going to spend the next few days unpacking this idea of reputation.

It's worth noting here, too, that Boaz has made a reputation for himself, as well. In verse 11, he talks about the people in the city as his people, so he has some kind of leadership in Bethlehem. Boaz also sits at the city gate among the elders of the city (Ruth 4:1-2). In chapter two, we saw how his servants respected him and the kindness with which he treated Ruth. He is a man of honorable character, and he agrees to redeem Ruth and Naomi, but he agrees to redeem them in accordance with the Mosaic Law. There is a closer relative to Naomi and Ruth than himself, and that man has the first right of redemption. Boaz agrees to go to the city gate the next morning to find out if the closest relative will redeem them. But if the closest relative would not redeem them, then Boaz promises that he will. Based on the character of Boaz that Ruth has witnessed already, she can have confidence that he will keep his word.

What kind of reputation had Ruth built for herself? Well, first, she left behind her old life in Moab to take care of Naomi and to worship Naomi's God instead of the gods of Moab. She has chosen the Lord above all else. She chose to press into God's way of life, even though it was an unknown path.

She worked hard to provide for herself and Naomi, demonstrating her selfless love, her commitment to her covenant with Naomi, and her strong work ethic.

Ruth had made a promise to Naomi in chapter one, but in the rest of the book we see her words lived out in her actions, proving to those around her that she was a woman of excellence who is trustworthy, kind, and submissive to her mother-in-law and ultimately the Lord.

Ruth's reputation is like what the end of Proverbs 31 speaks of:

Her children rise up and bless her; Her husband also, and he praises her, saying: "Many daughters have done nobly, But you excel them all." Charm is deceitful and beauty is vain, But a woman who fears the Lord, she shall be praised. Give her the product of her hands, And let her works praise her in the gates. Proverbs 31:28-31

Her good works are praising her in the gates, and Boaz has taken note of this. He has great respect for her and her godly reputation. We'll look more at this topic of reputation tomorrow.

STUDY: RUTH 3:6-13

Read today's passage and Proverbs 31:28-31 and mark any references to God in the passages.

Answer the following questions:

1: How does Ruth demonstrate humility and confidence in how she addresses Boaz?

2: What is Boaz's answer to Ruth? How does he demonstrate his godly character in this passage?

3: What kind of reputation does the Proverbs 31 woman have?

4: Read Deuteronomy 25:5-10. This is the law of the kinsman redeemer. How do Ruth and Boaz show respect for the law of God in how they are handling this matter?

Bonus: Read Ephesians 5:15-33. What do you learn about godly character and a godly marriage from this passage? How do Boaz and Ruth stack up against Paul's descriptions of a godly husband and wife?

DAY 3
Ruth 3:6-13

Today we are going to look more into the topic of reputation.

We live in a world of "self." Where it's all about you: you are the star. Selfies, Instagram, Snapchat, and the list goes on. Share you! It doesn't matter how silly, dumb, or inappropriate it is anymore. Not in this world. A huge message that we hear often is, "Don't worry about what others think of you. Just be yourself!" Even in Christian circles this message is proclaimed. "It doesn't matter what others think of you. Jesus still loves you no matter what. Just be yourself!" While to some degree this message is true, there's the other half of the equation I think we're forgetting. And it's found in the story of Ruth.

Ruth had a reputation for being a woman of *excellence*. Can you imagine what an honor that would be? And she was from Moab, an enemy country of Israel. Ruth had completely given up her old way of life and was choosing to walk in the ways of the Lord. She had laid down her own pursuits in order to care for her elderly mother-in-law, and people took note.

Your reputation is important.

While it is true that we aren't supposed to worry about what others think about us (but rather what God thinks of us), our reputations still matter. We are ambassadors for Christ (see 2 Corinthians 5:20) - we represent Him. Our reputations really aren't about us, but about our Lord.

Proverbs is full of admonitions to have a good reputation: "A good name is to be more desired than great wealth" (Prov. 22:1); the one who lives by kindness and truth "will find favor and good repute in the sight of God and man" (Prov. 3:1-4); "the memory of the righteous is blessed" (Prov. 10:7); the godly woman is praised by her husband and children and spoken well of in the gates (Prov. 31:28-31).

Reputation is important, but a good reputation should not be about stroking our pride or self-exaltation. While a good reputation brings honor to yourself and your family, that is not the main reason our reputation matters. For the Christian, a good reputation is about bringing glory to Jesus Christ.

Finally then, brethren, we request and exhort you in the Lord Jesus, that as you received from us instruction as to how you ought to walk and please God (just as you actually do walk), that you excel still more. 1 Thessalonians 4:1

Having a good reputation is not about bringing attention to yourself or gaining praise for yourself. We are to live for God and His glory alone. His opinion is the only one that matters, and He will judge the motives of our hearts that only He can see. We aren't supposed to practice our righteousness before men so that we can gain their praise; we are to live godly lives in the sight of God because He is a worthy Father (Matthew 6:1-6). As fallen humans, we will not be perfect in portraying Christ to the world around us, and our motives for godly living will not always be perfectly for God's glory and not our own. But praise the Lord for His grace! He will continue to sanctify our motives, our actions, and our reputations. Let us live for Him day by day, moment by moment, and for His glory alone.

STUDY: RUTH 3:6-13

Read today's passage and mark any references to God in the passage.

Answer the following questions:

1: In what ways does Ruth demonstrate that her godly living is for God's glory and not her own?

2: Read Prov. 3:1-4, Proverbs 10:7, Proverbs 22:1, Proverbs 31:28-31, and 2 Corinthians 5:20. What do you learn about a good reputation from these passages?

3: Read Matthew 6:1-6. How do we balance having a good reputation with doing our righteous deeds in secret?

4: Read Philippians 2:1-18. Paul urges the Philippians to be humble like Christ while also shining as lights in the world. How does this relate to our study on reputation?

DAY 4
Ruth 3:14-18

Today's passage starts with Boaz protecting and providing for Ruth once again. He protects her reputation by not allowing it to be spoken of that she came to the threshing floor, and he provides for her by sending her home to Naomi with six measures of barely. Boaz is again a picture of the care that Christ gives to His church in protecting and providing for her.

When Ruth returns to Naomi, she is anxious to know how everything went. After Ruth fills her in on everything that occurred, Naomi tells her, "Wait, my daughter, until you know how the matter turns out; for the man will not rest until he has settled it today" (Ruth 3:18).

The Hebrew word for "wait" here is yāšaḇ, which means "to sit down," "to dwell," or "to remain."[1] Naomi is telling Ruth to sit down, to rest, and to trust. She has done what she can do, and now the matter is in the Lord's hands. The women know they can trust Boaz to keep his word and settle the matter. They also know that God will do what is best for them.

It can be difficult to "sit down" and wait when we are really hoping for something to turn out a certain way. It's tempting to take matters into our own hands, to go beyond what we know the Lord has asked of us, and to try to manipulate circumstances to result in what we desire. But if we have done what the Lord has set before us, the best thing to do is to trust the Lord to bring about what He deems is best. He is a good God who will work in our lives to bring about our good and His glory. It may not always look the way we anticipate it to look, though.

Think of the life of Joseph. He went from being his father's favorite son to a slave in Egypt to a

44.

1: "H3427 – yāšaḇ – Strong's Hebrew Lexicon (nasb95)." Blue Letter Bible. Accessed 18 Feb, 2025. https://www.blueletterbible.org/lexicon/h3427/nasb95/wlc/0-6/#lexResults

prisoner in Egypt – all after having a prophetic dream of his brothers bowing down to him (see Genesis 37 & 39). I can imagine Joseph sitting in a prison cell wondering what the Lord was doing. Certainly, this was not how Joseph envisioned his life turning out back when he had his dream as a teenager. But in time, Joseph was promoted to a leadership position in Egypt and was used by God to save the lives of many people from famine, including his own family (Genesis 41-42). Joseph had several years of his life to wait and see what the Lord would do, and as he waited, he was faithful to serve the Lord in slavery, in prison, and in leadership. The Lord brought Joseph's dream to pass in a very unexpected way, but in a way that brought maximum glory to God.

Ruth's life probably wasn't turning out the way she had planned, either. She probably didn't expect her first husband to die young, nor did she expect to leave Moab and move to a foreign country and serve the God of the Israelites. But she surrendered to the Lord. She was faithful to serve Him with what was in front of her. And now she waits. As she trusted Him with the move to Bethlehem, now she trusts Him with providing a kinsman redeemer.

Life is full of waiting. But it is in the waiting that we learn to rest in the sovereignty and goodness of God. We learn that "none of those who wait for You will be ashamed" (Psalm 25:3). If we have Christ, we have all that we need, and we can rest knowing that if the Lord is asking us to wait, it is for our good (Psalm 84:11).

Sovereignty:
of God, his absolute right to do all things according to his own good pleasure (Dan 4:25,35; Rom 9:15-23; 1Ti 6:15; Rev 4:11).[1]

1: "Dictionaries - Sovereignty." Blue Letter Bible. Accessed 18 Feb, 2025. https://www.blueletterbible.org/search/Dictionary/viewTopic.cfm

STUDY: RUTH 3:14-18

Read today's passage and mark any references to God in the passage.

Answer the following questions:

1: How does Boaz send Ruth back to Naomi? In what ways is Boaz a "type" of Christ?
(A type is something in the Old Testament that gives a picture foreshadowing or pointing to Christ.)

2: Naomi tells Ruth to wait and see how things turn out. Why do you think she used the word yāšaḇ here?

3: Read Psalm 27:14, Psalm 84:11, Isaiah 40:31, and Romans 8:28. What do you learn about waiting on the Lord from these verses?

4: Read Genesis 50:20, Job 42:2, Proverbs 19:21, and Romans 11:36. How does knowing that God is in charge of everything impact our waiting on the Lord?

Bonus: Read the account of the life of Joseph (Genesis 37, 39-50). What connections do you draw between his life and Ruth's life? What do you learn about trusting God and His sovereignty from their stories?

DAY 5

Review Ruth 3:1-18

Read Ruth 3:1-18 and Proverbs 31:10-31 and spend some time meditating on the following questions:

1: What have I learned about God this week?

2: How does this chapter point to the gospel?

3: What have I learned about godly womanhood this week?

4: What has the Lord revealed to me through this chapter about how I ought to live?

5: How can I apply what I have learned from this chapter in this next week?

6: Journal a prayer to the Lord.

Now, my daughter, do not fear. I will do for you whatever you ask, for all my people in the city know that you are a woman of excellence.

Ruth 3:11

REPUTATION

WEEK FOUR:
REDEMPTION

DAY 1
Ruth 4:1-6

Chapter 4 begins with Boaz going to the city gate to settle the matter of redemption for Ruth and Naomi, just as he promised. He once again proves himself to be faithful.

Boaz calls aside the close relative of Naomi along with ten elders of the city, and he asks the close relative to redeem Elimelech's land, (Ruth 4:1-4). The Hebrew word for "redeem" is gā'al, which means "to be the next of kin (and as such to buy back a relative's property, marry his widow, etc.)."[1] Throughout the Mosaic Law, God gave specific instructions to close relatives regarding their care for one another, and a part of this care was being a redeemer. If a close relative became very poor and had to sell his land or sell himself into slavery, a kinsman redeemer would buy back the land or their close relative from slavery (Leviticus 25). A gā'al would also execute justice, or the death penalty, for a relative who had been murdered (Numbers 35:19). Boaz was calling upon the close relative to provide financially for Naomi, or to be her gā'al by buying Elimelech's land. And the close relative agrees to do this.

But then Boaz calls upon the close relative to fulfill one more duty required of a close relative. He reminds the close relative that not only was he to buy back the land, he would also need to raise up an heir to carry on Elimelech's name, as the Law required (Deuteronomy 25:5-6). At this point, the close relative says he cannot be a gā'al for Ruth and Naomi because it would "jeopardize my own inheritance," and he tells Boaz to be the redeemer (Ruth 4:6). Scripture doesn't specify why the man's inheritance would be jeopardized by this; we can assume he had a wife and children already, and having a second wife and more children would complicate

1: "H1350 - gā'al - Strong's Hebrew Lexicon (nasb95)." Blue Letter Bible. Accessed 19 Feb, 2025. https://www.blueletterbible.org/lexicon/h1350/nasb95/wlc/0-1/

matters greatly (and, since the beginning of creation, God's pattern for marriage has been one man and one woman for life; any time people deviated from God's design for marriage in the Old Testament, we see it came with much pain and heartbreak).

Boaz now has the right under the Law to be the kinsman redeemer for Ruth and Naomi now that the closer relative has ceded his right to Boaz (this will be sealed in verse 8). God blessed Boaz's faithfulness to obey the Law regarding close relatives. We can always trust God with the outcome of our obedience to Him.

The theme of redemption is significant in the book of Ruth, but it points to an even greater theme running throughout the whole Bible. Ruth and Naomi were poor widows; they had nothing to their names. They could not provide security for themselves. But Boaz stepped in as a redeemer to provide them security, provision, and a name.

Humanity is like Ruth and Naomi - we are poor, broken sinners with nothing to our names. Worse than Naomi and Ruth, we are slaves of sin. We worship the god of self and call upon this god to raise us up from our pit of destruction, not realizing that we are chained to our self-made gods. We cannot free ourselves. Worse still, we are like the murderer the gā'al has a right to destroy: we have all sinned against a holy God, and the just punishment for that sin is death (Rom. 6:23). We do not deserve a redeemer.

But Christ, in His glorious grace, stepped down from heaven, took on human flesh, and humbled Himself to the point of death on a cross in our place (Phil. 2:5-8). He paid the price required to free us, the slaves held captive by sin. He bought us back at the price of His own blood, despite our wretchedness. Despite the sin we had committed in defiance of the Holy One. Despite the fact that we were enemies of God. He bought us back. And not only that, He purifies us by His blood and imputes His righteousness to us, giving us a new name. And because of our new name in Christ, we have an inheritance as children of God (see Ephesians 1).

The redemption of Ruth by Boaz is a beautiful story, but it points to an even more beautiful, jaw-dropping story: the story of Jesus Christ, the Savior of the world, our Redeemer. May we forever stand in awe of His glorious grace.

Redeem:

"to buy back," "to free from what distresses or harms," "to change for the better," "to exchange for something of value," "to atone for." [1]

Redeemer:

"one charged with the duty of restoring the rights of another and avenging his wrongs. This title is peculiarly applied to Christ. He redeems us from all evil by the payment of a ransom." [2]

1: "Definition of REDEEM." n.d. Www.merriam-Webster.com. https://www.merriam-webster.com/dictionary/redeem.

2: Easton, M. "Redeemer - Easton's Bible Dictionary." Blue Letter Bible. Last Modified 24 Jun, 1996. https://www.blueletterbible.org/search/Dictionary/viewTopic.cfm

STUDY: RUTH 4:1-6

Read today's passage and mark any references to God in the passage.

Answer the following questions:

1: What do you learn about Boaz from today's passage?

2: Read the following passages about the gā'al: Leviticus 25:23-55 and Deuteronomy 25:5-6. What does this context teach you about Ruth and Naomi's situation? What clarity does it provide for Boaz and the close relative's conversation?

3: Read the following verses: Romans 3:21-26, Galatians 3:13, Ephesians 1:13-14, Hebrews 9:11-12, and 1 Peter 1:17-19. What do you learn about Christ as our redeemer?

4: The close relative mentions his inheritance in verse 6. Read the following verses: Acts 20:32, Ephesians 1:18-21, and 1 Peter 1:3-5. What do you learn about our inheritance as believers?

Bonus: Take a look at the book of Hosea. What do you learn about redemption from this book? (As a quick overview: the Lord instructed Hosea to take a harlot for a wife. She ran away from him to continue living as a harlot, but he bought her back. God used this relationship to show Hosea, and us, what He sees when His creation rebels against Him continually. But, like Hosea redeemed Gomer even though she didn't deserve it, God redeemed us through Christ. This book is worth taking extra time to read through!)

DAY 2
Ruth 4:7-12

The close relative has agreed to give Boaz his right of redemption. To seal this exchange, the man removed his sandal and gave it to Boaz (Ruth 4:7-8). In Deuteronomy 25, if a close relative refused to be a kinsman redeemer and raise up the name of the deceased (which means taking the widow for his wife, and their first son would take on the deceased's name), then the widow would take the relative before the elders. If he refused to do his duty, he would remove his sandal, and the widow would spit in his face to symbolize his dishonor. Here in Ruth, the man removed his sandal, but because he relinquished his rights to Boaz, there would not be dishonor for him. The widows would still be cared for according to God's design.

It's good to note here that the Lord, in His Law, made provisions for caring for those in need. It was the role of the extended family to care for their own, but when that was not available, God still provided for their needs by allowing widows to glean in the corners of the fields, as we learned earlier in this study. It's important, as believers, to remember the responsibility we have before God to care for our family members and also the body of Christ. Just as God had means for providing for the needy in Israel, the Lord instructs His church to care for her needy members as well.

Boaz stands before the elders and people and calls on them to be witnesses to what has happened: he is taking full responsibility for Naomi and Ruth and taking upon himself the role of kinsman redeemer (Ruth 4:9-10). Boaz is not taking this role flippantly; he is calling upon the people of Bethlehem to hold him accountable to his word. He will redeem Elimelech's land and marry Ruth in order to raise up Elimelech's name on his inheritance.

The people respond, agreeing to be witnesses and giving Boaz a blessing (Ruth 4:11-12). They pray that the Lord will give Boaz and Ruth many children, that He will provide wealth and fame to Boaz in Bethlehem, and that their house would make a name for themselves like Perez (this seemingly random mention of Perez, the child of Tamar and Judah, is the ancestor of the Bethlehemites, which might explain why the people include Perez in their blessing for Boaz).[1]

Boaz's interaction with the people and elders of Bethlehem is a good reminder of the importance of both the promises we make and the accountability we have in our lives. Like Ruth in chapter one, Boaz is making a solemn oath before the Lord, and the Lord takes our promises seriously. God is always faithful to His word, and His standard of righteousness is the standard by which we ought to conduct our lives. But we are prone to fail at keeping our word. We forget; we get lazy; we make excuses. One of the best ways we can set ourselves up for success is to have accountability for our promises. This is one of the reasons we have marriage ceremonies in front of an audience. It's not just because we want to share our special moment with loved ones; we are calling upon the congregation to be witnesses to the vows we are taking before God. The congregation then has the responsibility to hold the married couple accountable to their vows through sunshine and rain.

Boaz becomes the redeemer for Ruth and Naomi and was willing to marry Ruth, even though she was a Moabitess, one of the enemies of Israel. Boaz, again, shows us a picture of Jesus as our Redeemer. Genesis 3 tells the account of the fall, or humanity's first sin. The sins of Adam and all the world have separated us from God and brought death into the world, just like leaving Bethlehem brought death into Elimelech's family. But in Jesus, we have been given the free gift of God's grace, righteousness, salvation, and eternal life. In a way, we are all like Ruth; before we accepted Jesus, we were enemies of God like the Moabites were to Israel. But God showed us His great love in that while we were still His enemies, Christ died on the cross for us. And because of His free gift, we become a part of God's family, just like Ruth became a part of Boaz's family and a part of the lineage of Christ. There are so many great lessons to learn in studying the book of Ruth, but the greatest lesson is that our Kinsman Redeemer is Someone greater than Boaz - it's Jesus. And His redemption is available to everyone who will call on His name.

1: Guzik, D. "Study Guide for Ruth 4 by David Guzik." Blue Letter Bible. Last Modified 6/2022. https://www.blueletterbible.org/comm/guzik_david/study-guide/ruth/ruth-4.cfm

STUDY: RUTH 4:7-12

Read today's passage and mark any references to God in the passage.

Answer the following questions:

1: What vow does Boaz take before the people after receiving the sandal that signified his willingness to redeem Naomi and Ruth?

2: What blessing do the elders and people give Ruth and Boaz? How does this blessing reflect how the city views Ruth, the Moabitess?

3: The close relative gave Boaz his sandal as a sign. Read the following verses: 2 Corinthians 1:21-22, Ephesians 1:13-14, Ephesians 4:30, and 2 Timothy 2:19. What sign has the Lord given concerning His pledge of redemption to us?

4: What other significant promises can you think of in Scripture? How did the people demonstrate the seriousness of their promises or covenants? What insight does this give you for promises we make today?

DAY 3
Ruth 4:13-15 &
Proverbs 31:23-31

Boaz kept his word and took Ruth as his wife, and the Lord blessed them with a son, Obed. God again shows Himself to be present in Ruth and Naomi's life, providing them with not only security in Boaz but a future in Obed.

The women of Bethlehem take note of all God has done for Naomi and bless God for His faithful and loving care of Naomi. Naomi, who had told the women to call her Mara because the Lord's hand was against her, has learned that her Heavenly Father was never against her. God has blessed her beyond her wildest dreams.

The women of the city also tell Naomi that God has blessed her with a daughter-in-law who loves her and is better to her than seven sons (Ruth 4:15). Ruth's reputation has once again preceded her. Her love for Naomi is evident throughout Bethlehem. And she is better to Naomi than seven sons. Seven was the number of days it took for the Lord to create the world, and it is symbolic of completion. So, the women are telling Naomi that Ruth is even better than a perfect number of sons. That is high praise!

Ruth is again living up to the Proverbs 31 woman. Her works are praising her throughout Bethlehem (Prov. 31:31). Her new husband is known among the gates (Prov. 31:23). She has looked after Naomi with great love (Prov. 31:27). She has proven herself to be a woman who fears the Lord, and she is praised by the people of Bethlehem (Prov. 31:30).

Ruth and Naomi have so much they can praise the Lord for. They didn't know how the Lord would work things out for them, and He did above and beyond what they expected. Naomi expected condemnation; God gave grace. Naomi expected childlessness; God gave her a daughter-in-law and a grandson. Naomi expected poverty; God gave security. Naomi expected desolation; God gave a redeemer. Naomi expected death; God brought life.

Naomi learns, through the faithfulness of God, that she can smile at the future (Prov. 31:25). The future is full of unknowns. It is something we cannot control, and because of that most of us tend to fear what the future will bring. But through the events of her life, Naomi has seen that the future is held in the hands of a faithful God. And this God is not a fierce hand waiting to crush her; this is the hand of a loving Father who allows hardships in our lives to shape us and directs the paths of our lives by His grace, providing for us what we need for when we need it. Will the future hold hardships? Quite possibly. But will our Father's hand ever let us go? Never.

God is full of grace, mercy, and compassion, and that is evident in the lives of Naomi and Ruth. We may not always see what He is working in our lives, but we can trust that it will be for His glory and our good. The greatest grace, mercy, and compassion He showed was at the cross, and for all eternity we will be praising His glorious grace.

STUDY: RUTH 4:13-15
& PROVERBS 31:23-31

Read today's passages and mark any references to God in the passages.

Answer the following questions:

1: How does God's faithfulness shine in Ruth 4?

2: Read the following verses: Numbers 23:19, Deuteronomy 7:9, Psalm 36:5, Lamentations 3:22-23, 1 Corinthians 1:9, 2 Timothy 2:13. What do you learn about God's faithfulness?

3: What does it mean to smile at the future? Why do you think this is listed as a characteristic of a woman who fears the Lord?

4: Read the following verses: Proverbs 3:5-6, Jeremiah 29:11, Nahum 1:7, Matthew 6:25-33, Romans 8:28 & 38-39, 1 Peter 5:7. What do they teach you about trusting the Lord with the future?

DAY 4
Ruth 4:16-22

Things have come full circle for Naomi. She lost her two sons, but now the Lord has blessed her with a grandson, and she gets to be his nurse. The neighbor women are so excited to see how God has given Naomi beauty for ashes, and they name Ruth's baby Obed, which means "serving" or "worshipping."[1] The Lord provided abundantly for Naomi's needs, and the only proper response to His grace is worship. Obed would forever be a reminder to worship the Lord for His faithfulness.

The book of Ruth concludes with a genealogy, starting with Perez, who, as we learned before, was the ancestor of the Bethlehemites. This genealogy leads to King David, the great-grandson of Ruth, setting up the book to lead right into the books of 1 and 2 Samuel which chronicle the life of David. And, a little over a thousand years later, a descendant of Ruth would journey to Bethlehem from Nazareth for a census and there give birth to the Son of David who was prophesied to sit on David's throne forever: Jesus Christ. From the House of Bread would come the Bread of Life. Take a look at some of the other ways Jesus shows up in the book of Ruth:[2]

- The kinsman-redeemer had to be a relative; Jesus took on humanity to become our kinsman.
- Just as the kinsman-redeemer bought family out of slavery, Jesus bought us out of slavery to sin and death.
- The kinsman-redeemer bought back the land of his relatives; Jesus is redeeming back the world that was forfeited to the devil.
- Boaz was motivated by selfless love for Ruth; Jesus redeemed us out of His great love.
- Boaz had a plan to redeem Ruth; Jesus had a plan to redeem us from the before time began.

1: "Dictionaries - Obed." Blue Letter Bible. Accessed 20 Feb, 2025. https://www.blueletterbible.org/search/Dictionary/viewTopic.cfm

2: Guzik, D. "Study Guide for Ruth 4 by David Guzik." Blue Letter Bible. Last Modified 6/2022. https://www.blueletterbible.org/comm/guzik_david/study-guide/ruth/ruth-4.cfm

- Boaz took Ruth as his bride; the church, whom Christ redeemed, will be His bride.
- Boaz provided Ruth with a future; Jesus provides us with a glorious, eternal future with Himself.

David Guzik summarizes it well in his Ruth study guide:

> "But it all comes back to the idea of Jesus as our kinsman-redeemer; this is why He became a man. God might have sent an angel to save us, but the angel would not have been our kinsman. Jesus, in His eternal glory, without the addition of humanity to His divine nature might have saved us, but He would not have been our kinsman. A great prophet or priest would be our kinsman, but his own sin would have disqualified him as our redeemer. Only Jesus, the eternal God who added humanity to His eternal deity, can be both the kinsman and the redeemer for mankind!... From eternity, God planned to bring Ruth and Boaz together, and thus make Bethlehem His entrance point for the coming of Jesus as our true Kinsman-Redeemer, fully God and fully man." [1]

As we wrap up our study of the book of Ruth, I pray that you walk away in awe of God's faithfulness. I pray that you have renewed confidence in the hand of a Father who will never leave you. I pray that you will partake of the Bread of Life that your Kinsman Redeemer has given you. And may our response to His gift be worship and service to our King for all eternity.

1: Guzik, D. "Study Guide for Ruth 4 by David Guzik." ©1996-present The Enduring Word Bible Commentary by David Guzik - enduringword.com. Used with permission.

STUDY: RUTH 4:16-22

Read today's passage and mark any references to God in the passage.

Answer the following questions:

1: How did God set the stage for King David through the story of Ruth? For the coming of the Messiah?

2: Why does the Bible contain genealogies? What do we learn from the lists of names in Scripture? In the book of Ruth?

3: The neighbor women name Ruth's son Obed, which means "serving" or "worshipping." Based on everything we've learned so far, why do you think they chose that name for Obed?

4: Write out a prayer to the Lord, thanking Him for His sovereign hand over history.

Bonus: The genealogy of Christ listed in Matthew 1 specifically lists five women. Read through Matthew 1 and write down the names of these five women. Then, do a little digging into their lives. Who were they? What makes them significant? Why are they specifically listed in the genealogy of Christ?

DAY 5

Review Ruth 4:1-22

Read Ruth 4:1-22 and Proverbs 31:10-31 and spend some time meditating on the following questions:

1: What have I learned about God this week?

2: How does this chapter point to the gospel?

3: What have I learned about godly womanhood this week?

4: What has the Lord revealed to me through this chapter about how I ought to live?

5: How can I apply what I have learned from this chapter in this next week?

6: Journal a prayer to the Lord.

Then the women said to Naomi, "Blessed is the Lord who has not left you without a redeemer today, and may his name become famous in Israel. May he also be to you a restorer of life and a sustainer of your old age; for your daughter-in-law, who loves you and is better to you than seven sons, has given birth to him."

Ruth 4:14-15

REDEMPTION

Conclusion

I hope this Bible study encouraged you, challenged you, and gave you a vision for living as a woman of excellence. Living for the glory of God as a woman is not popular these days, but as we allow the Holy Spirit to sanctify and grow us toward godliness, we will find it to be more than worth it! Most importantly, I hope this study filled you with awe and thankfulness for our Kinsman Redeemer, Jesus Christ.

May the Lord bless you as you continue to pursue Him each day. May you continue to grow in the knowledge of Christ, and may He be glorified in you!

Let's connect!
www.kelseyleewrites.com
Instagram: @kelseyleewrites
Facebook: KelseyGjesdalAuthor
Tiktok: @kelsey.lee.writes

In Christ,

KELSEY LEE

Resources from Kelsey Lee Writes LLC

Subscribe to my author newsletter to stay up-to-date on all of the latest news with Kelsey Lee Writes LLC and receive a FREE 3-day devotional based on my book series, *the Truth Squad Trilogy:*

> https://kelseyleewritesllc.kit.com/allindevotional

Check out my website, kelseyleewrites.com, where I share a monthly devotional about what the Lord is teaching me. There, you will also find my shop for future resources like this one and links to purchase my books.

Check out my podcast, Wholeheartedly with Kelsey Lee. This podcast is dedicated to encouraging young adults to know why they believe what they believe and to let the Word of God impact every aspect of life. Two new episodes drop every month! Available wherever you listen to podcasts.

Check out my teen mystery series, *The Truth Squad Trilogy*! Follow along with friends Rebecca, Sarah, and Luke as they overcome their own inner turmoil and fight against an evil take-over operation. You can find *Third Identity*, *Second Thoughts*, and *First Priority* at your favorite online retailers.

Coming soon!
Fiction:
• *Grandpa's Comrade*: Siblings Jess and Will go on an unexpected adventure to Korea when Grandpa's MIA comrade sends him a mysterious wooden box. Can the teens help Grandpa find his comrade before time runs out?

Non-fiction:
• *Mindset: Learning to Live with the Mind of Christ. A 60-Day Study through the book of Philippians* (in production!)
• *Everyday Theology: What Theology Is and Why it Matters to Gen-Z* (working title)

* 9 7 9 8 9 9 9 1 6 2 7 0 0 *